Dedicated to all
Dispatchers and
their families.

Thank You.

To have a Dispatcher in your family!

Why is that, you may ask?
Well, the answer is clear...

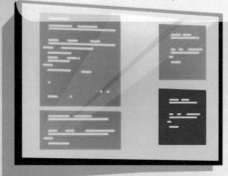

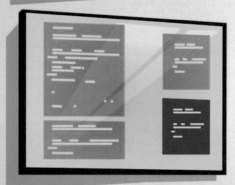

Dispatchers help people every day of every year.

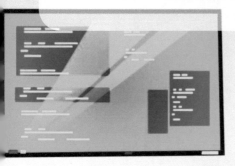

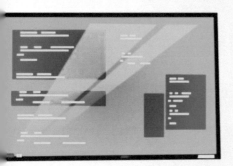
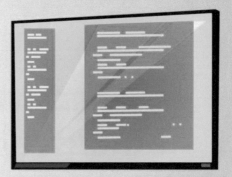

A dispatcher is a hero, with a strong mind and a caring heart...

And whenever there is an emergency, dispatchers play a very important part!

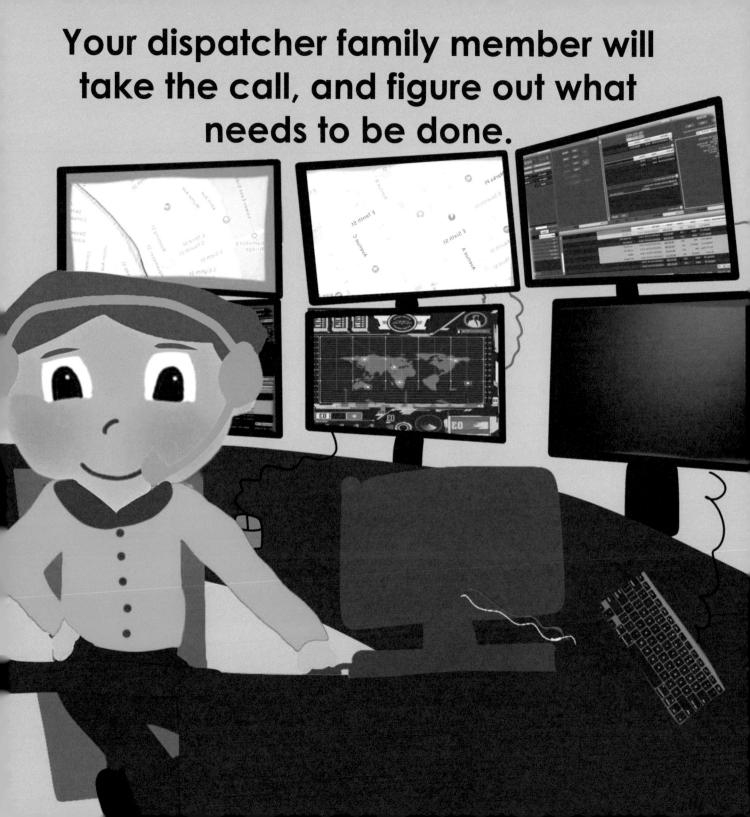

They'll get the callers information, and send first responders on the way.

They stay calm on the phone to assure the caller that everything will be okay.

Dispatchers may even have to instruct a caller on things they have to do...

Like how to provide medical care,
and many more things too!

When Dispatchers go to work,
they'll have a lot to do…

But all throughout their shift, they will be thinking about you!

Sometimes your Dispatcher family member has to work on a holiday, or miss a special event...

The 911 calls always need to be answered, but they sure wish they could have went!

But they cannot miss work when there's so many people that need help, and so much to do!

See the thing with Dispatchers is
that they are needed
all the time...

Because people call 911 if they need help, are hurt, are in trouble, or if they see a crime!

But after work when the
day is through...

**Your dispatcher family member
cannot wait to come
home to you!**

And as soon as they get back home when their shift is done...

Do you know what your Dispatcher
family member's favorite thing is to do?

You guessed it right...
their favorite thing is being with you!

Whether they are far or near,
their love is always there...

In fact, Dispatchers have so much love, it will be with you everywhere!

So always remember
how lucky you are

To have a Dispatcher family member
who loves you near and far!

Made in United States
Troutdale, OR
11/07/2024

24547914R00021